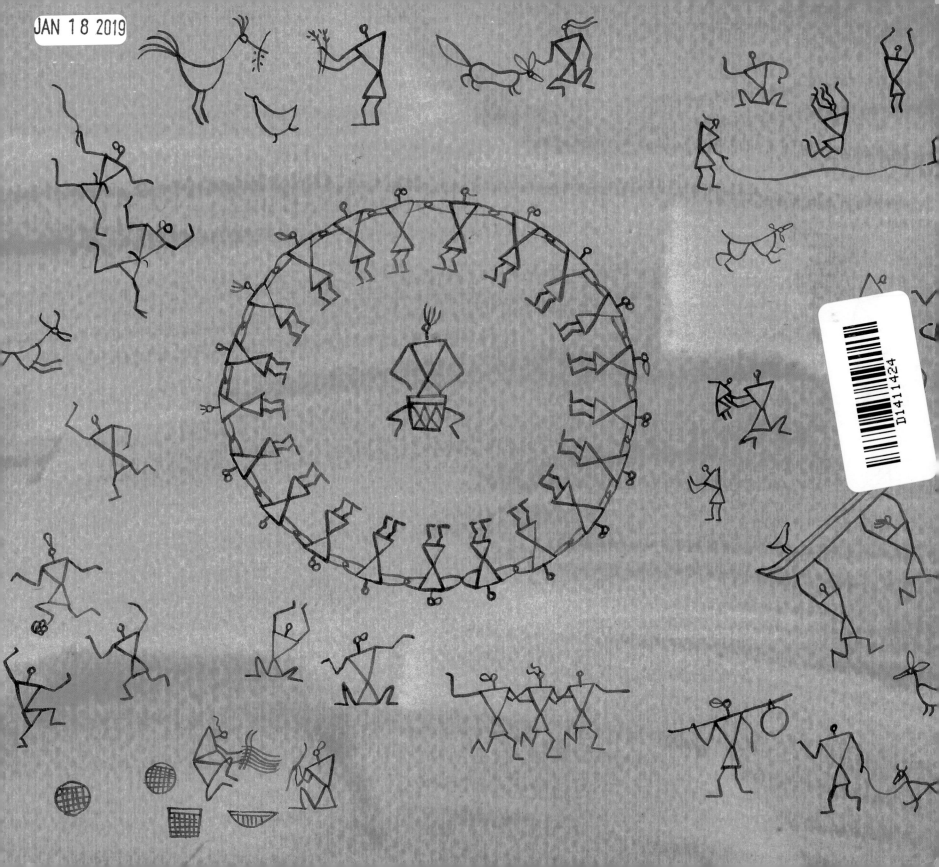

This English edition published in 2017 under license from big & SMALL
by Eerdmans Books for Young Readers,
an imprint of Wm. B. Eerdmans Publishing Co.
2140 Oak Industrial Dr. NE, Grand Rapids, Michigan 49505
www.eerdmans.com/youngreaders

Original Korean text by Hye-eun Shin • Illustrations by Su-bi Jeong • English edition edited by Joy Cowley
Original Korean edition © Yeowon Media Co., Ltd. • English edition © big & SMALL 2014

17 18 19 20 21 22 23   9 8 7 6 5 4 3 2 1

Manufactured at Tien Wah Press in Malaysia

Names: Shin, Hye-eun, author. | Jeong, Su-Bi, illustrator. | Cowley, Joy,
  editor.
Title: The Warli people / by Hye-eun Shin ; illustrated by Su-bi Jeong ;
  edited by Joy Cowley.
Description: Grand Rapids, MI : Eerdmans Books for Young Readers, [2017] |
  Audience: Ages 6-10.
Identifiers: LCCN 2017000496 | ISBN 9780802854766
Subjects: LCSH: Warli (Indic people)—Juvenile literature. | Warli (Indic
  people)—Agriculture—Juvenile literature.
Classification: LCC DS432.W3 S54 2017 | DDC 934/.7901—dc23 LC record available at
https://lccn.loc.gov/2017000496

Display type set in Blue Highway Linocut
Text type set in Garamond

The Warli People

Written by **Hye-eun Shin**
Illustrated by **Su-bi Jeong**
Edited by **Joy Cowley**

Eerdmans Books for Young Readers

Grand Rapids, Michigan

Tribe

In about the 10th century BCE, in western India,
there lived a group of people called the Warlis.
The women in the Warli tribe drew pictures
on the walls of their mud-brick houses.
Drawing pictures was a sacred ritual for Warli people.

Spring

When spring arrived,
the Warli people
worked in their fields
along the banks of the river.

Planting Seeds

At the beginning of each new year,
the Warli people held a ceremony
to honor the land,
and then they planted seeds.
The seeds were scattered
over the fields and
covered with fresh earth.

Hunting

When the men went into the forest,
the animals ran away,
but the men chased them.
Animals provided meat for the people
to eat with their grain.

Getting Salt

The Warli people who lived by the sea
also caught and ate fish.
They made salt from sun-dried seawater,
and gathered it in baskets.
Salt was thought of as white treasure.

The Forest

The children played in the forest,
gathering flowers and fruit,
and chasing monkeys
and other small animals.

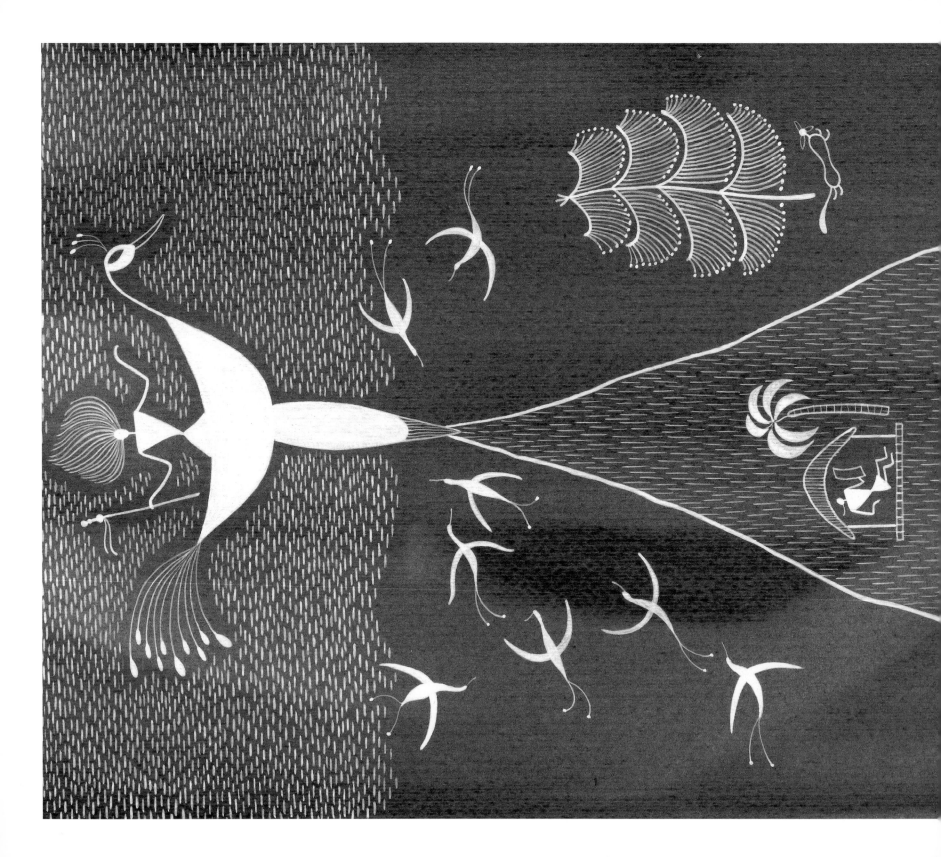

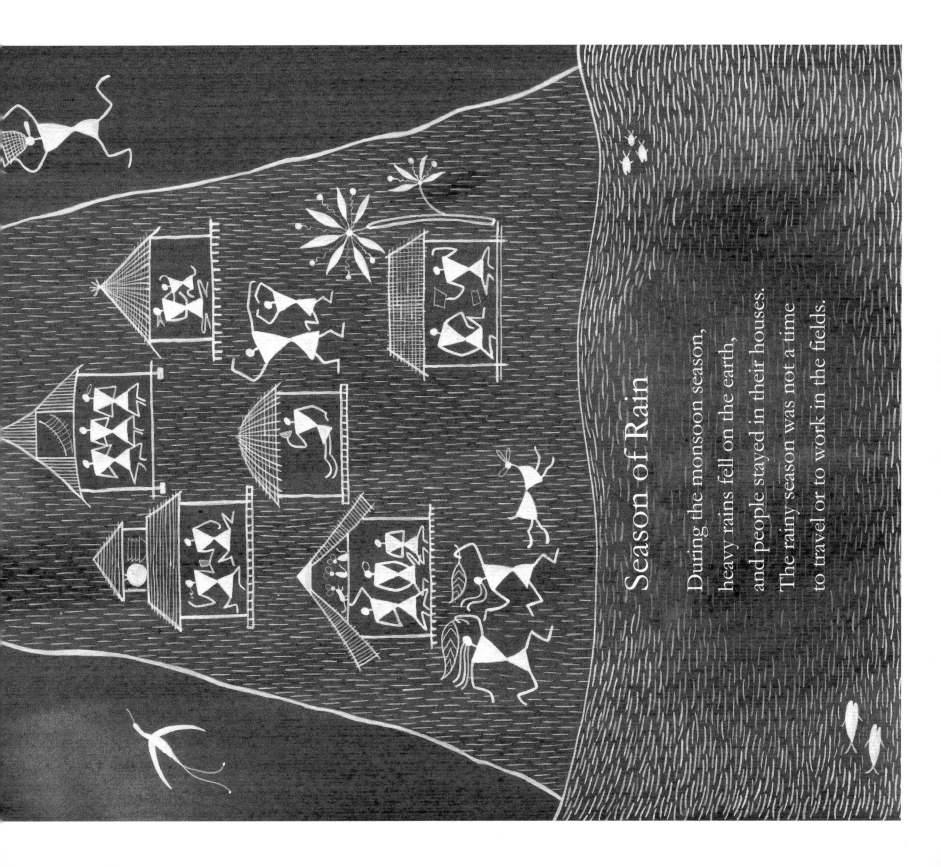

Season of Rain

During the monsoon season,
heavy rains fell on the earth,
and people stayed in their houses.
The rainy season was not a time
to travel or to work in the fields.

New Life

After the rain, the streams were full of water,
and the river flowed to the sea.
New life came to the land
after the summer monsoons.

Animals and Trees

The rain renewed the forest,
and there was food for the animals:
fresh green leaves, grass, and fruit.
Birds nested in the trees,
and animals gave birth.

The Village at Night

When the sun went down
and the moon rose in the sky,
the Warli people shared food,
made baskets and cloth,
and told stories before going to bed.

Harvest Time

The crops were ready.
The people harvested their grain
and rice and carried it to their village.
They now had food for the
coming year.

Food for the Year

The grain and the stalks
were separated by beating them.
The grain was stored,
and the stalks were fed to the animals.
Some of the grain was kept as seed
for new crops.

Festival Night

After the food was harvested,
the Warli people had a festival.
They danced and sang all night,
celebrating the generosity
of the good earth.

Wedding Day

The bride and groom rode a horse
leading a wedding procession.
They were married in the temple,
and everyone celebrated the
beginning of a new family.
The Warli people continued with their lives.

The Warli People

The Warlis lived on the western coast of India in what is now the state of Maharashtra. The earliest records of their existence date back to around 2500 BCE. During that time, civilizations in many areas of the world were shifting from hunting and gathering to farming. The Warli people were no exception.

Before the rise of farming, people were nomads, moving constantly to find sources of food. But as they learned how to raise animals and grow crops, they started to settle into communities. Each of these communities was founded on an agricultural economy — nearly everyone had a job related to farming. As farming techniques improved, these ancient groups of people — including the Warlis — could produce more food than they needed, gaining wealth and stability from the excess production.

Once people were able to settle in one place with access to reliable food sources, the population increased. Small farming communities became villages, towns, and eventually cities. This led to the development of more complex economies and lifestyles. Today, very few parts of the world still have a traditional agricultural economy. The agricultural economies of the Warlis and other ancient civilizations established the foundation for the modern economy and global trade.

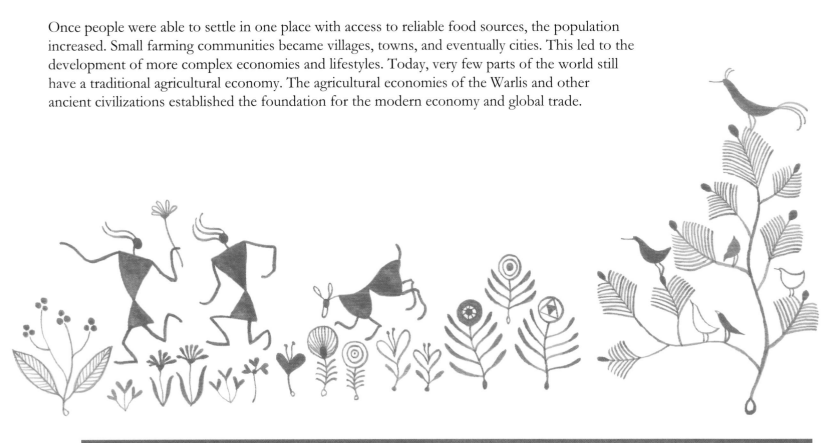

Key Terms and Concepts

A **hunter-gatherer** is a person living in a community that obtains food through hunting, fishing, and harvesting wild vegetation. Even though the Warlis were an agricultural society, they still used hunting and gathering for additional sources of food.

During the **harvest** season, the Warlis would gather the crops they grew and store them to eat in the coming months.

India's **monsoon** season occurs every year from June to October, bringing heavy rainfall to the area. Without this rain, the region's crops would not survive the summer heat.

In an **agricultural economy**, the people's way of life depends heavily on farming. Most jobs in an agricultural economy are rooted in farming and ranching.

The Rise of Civilization

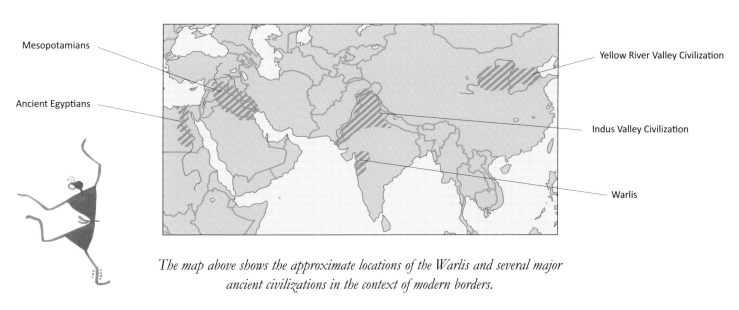

The map above shows the approximate locations of the Warlis and several major ancient civilizations in the context of modern borders.

Fresh water is vital to human life and necessary for farming and agriculture. The Warlis lived near several rivers, most notably the Ulhas River, which flows into the Arabian Sea. Many other ancient civilizations settled near rivers as well. The Indus Valley Civilization flourished along the banks of the Indus River, which flows through modern-day Pakistan. The Yellow River Valley was the cradle of Chinese civilization. The ancient Egyptians, who lived in a desert climate, relied on the waters of the Nile. And Mesopotamia, the fertile land between the Tigris and Euphrates Rivers, was home to multiple civilizations throughout history, including the Sumerians, Babylonians, and Assyrians.

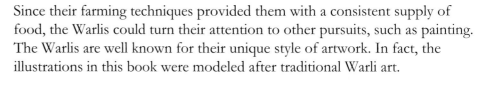

Since their farming techniques provided them with a consistent supply of food, the Warlis could turn their attention to other pursuits, such as painting. The Warlis are well known for their unique style of artwork. In fact, the illustrations in this book were modeled after traditional Warli art.

Warli artwork consists of geometric shapes made with a white rice flour paste on a darker background. Circles symbolize the sun and moon, squares indicate enclosed spaces, and an inverted triangle on top of another triangle represents a person. But the most important aspect of Warli artwork is that it does not depict mythological characters or deities, but rather day-to-day activities.

Since the lives of the Warli people were strongly linked to agriculture, nature is featured prominently in much of their artwork. Warli paintings often depict people fishing, farming, hunting, and harvesting. The Warlis also had a very close-knit community, so many of their paintings focus on their social life as well. Their artwork portrays important events, such as festivals, dances, and marriages. Warli paintings are admired not just for their beauty but for the insights they offer into the everyday life of the Warlis.

A Timeline of Events

A History of Early Farming

(Due to the limited information we have about these ancient times, these dates are approximations.)

8500 BCE	Cattle are domesticated in the Middle East.
8000 BCE	Mesopotamians start planting wheat and barley.
7000 BCE	People in China begin cultivating rice.
6000 BCE	Potatoes are first cultivated near the Andes in what is now Peru.
5000 – 4000 BCE	Agriculture spreads throughout Europe.
4000 – 3000 BCE	Horses are first domesticated in central Asia.
3500 BCE	The wheel and plow are invented in Mesopotamia.
3100 BCE	The first major irrigation project begins in Egypt, using the Nile River.
2100 BCE	People begin growing maize (corn) in what is now the southwest United States.